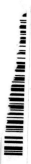

TEEN LIFE™

FREQUENTLY ASKED QUESTIONS ABOUT

Hate Crimes

Barbara Dunkell
and
Janell Broyles

ROSEN
PUBLISHING®

New York

Published in 2012 by The Rosen Publishing Group, Inc.
29 East 21st Street, New York, NY 10010

Library of Congress Cataloging-in-Publication Data

Dunkell, Barbara.
Frequently asked questions about hate crimes/Barbara Dunkell, Janell Broyles.
      p. cm.—(FAQ: teen life)
Includes bibliographical references and index.
ISBN 978-1-4488-5562-9 (library binding)
1. Hate crimes—Juvenile literature.
2. Hate crimes—United States—Juvenile literature.
I. Broyles, Janell. II. Title.
HV6773.5.D86 2012
364.15—dc22

                                                                2011015910

Manufactured in China

CPSIA Compliance Information: Batch #W12YA: For further information, contact Rosen Publishing, New York, New York, at 1-800-237-9932.

Contents

one

WHAT IS THE DEFINITION OF "HATE CRIME"?

According to an article in February 2011, posted on the College of Criminal Justice and Security Web site at the University of Phoenix in Arizona, one of the chief issues concerning hate crimes is the definition of what constitutes a hate crime. In a report, Rose Ochi, director of Community Relations Services in the U.S. Department of Justice, wrote that hate crime is described as "the violence of intolerance and bigotry, intended to hurt and intimidate someone because of their race, ethnicity, national origin, religion, sexual orientation or disability." She also stated that those who commit hate crimes "use explosives, arson, weapons, vandalism, physical violence, and verbal threats of violence to instill fear in their victims."

Hate is a universal human emotion. It is an extreme rejection of another person, the desire to have nothing to do with that person, and sometimes, the desire to hurt or

Teens surround a victim during a bias attack. According to the Federal Bureau of Investigation, of the 7,789 hate crimes that were reported in 2009, 61 percent were offenses committed against individuals.

kill that person. Everyone feels hate at some point in their lives, but most people choose not to lash out or are taught that it is wrong to use violence against others.

Hate crimes arise when a person or a group decides to act on hatred of another person or a group in a criminal way.

Hate Crime Laws

Some groups oppose the existence of hate crime laws, maintaining that regular laws against assault and violence protect all citizens, regardless of their color, ethnicity, religious beliefs, gender, or sexual orientation. Consequently, they believe, a special category of crime is not needed as further protection.

When the New York State legislature enacted the Hate Crimes Act of 2000, however, it found the following:

> Hate crimes do more than threaten the safety and welfare of all citizens . . . Hate crimes can and do intimidate and disrupt entire communities . . . Current law does not adequately recognize the harm to public order and individual safety that hate crimes cause. Therefore, our laws must be strengthened to provide clear recognition of the gravity of hate crimes and the compelling importance of preventing their recurrence. Accordingly, the legislature finds and declares that hate crimes should be prosecuted and punished with appropriate severity.

In 1993, the U.S. Supreme Court upheld the value of hate crime laws in *Wisconsin v. Mitchell*, a case involving a white youth beaten by a group of African Americans because of his race. The Supreme Court ruled that a state may consider whether a crime was committed or initially considered due to an intended victim's status in a protected class, such as race.

The International Association of Chiefs of Police (IACP) defines hate crimes in the following way: "A hate crime is a criminal offense committed against persons, property, or society that is motivated, in whole or in part, by an offender's bias against an individual's or a group's race, religion, ethnic/national origin, gender, age, disability, or sexual orientation." The IACP definition is the one most widely used, according to many police departments. Although it is a comprehensive hate crime definition, the IACP definition is only one definition. In U.S. federal laws, in state laws, and in international laws, hate crimes will vary in whom they include. Some differ in whether or not they include groups such as gays and lesbians, women, or the disabled, among other distinctions.

U.S. Federal Hate Crime Laws

U.S. Title 18, U.S.C., Section 245 makes it "unlawful to willfully injure, intimidate, or interfere with any person, or to attempt to do so, by force or threat of force, because of that other person's race, color, religion, or national origin." This law also protects against discrimination or harm to anyone who goes to a public school or college, travels around the country, uses government programs, works for the U.S. government, applies to a labor union or employment agency, is a juror, is engaging in a federally protected act such as voting, or goes into a public place like a movie theater or hotel. Punishment can range from imprisonment up to a life term or the death penalty, depending on the circumstances of the crime.

The Civil Rights Program of the Federal Bureau of Investigation (FBI) reports on its Web site (http://www. fbi.gov/about-us/investigate/civilrights/civil_rights) that a hate crime is not considered a distinct federal offense. If it is racially motivated, however, it can be considered a civil rights violation, which does fall under the FBI's jurisdiction. Although state and local authorities handle most hate crime cases, FBI investigations can often provide extra weight and authority to local cases. A 1994 federal law also increased penalties for offenses proven to be hate crimes.

President Barack Obama applauds the sisters of James Byrd Jr. and the parents of Matthew Shepard after the enactment of the Matthew Shepard and James Byrd Jr. Hate Crimes Prevention Act in 2009.

In 2009, the U.S. Congress passed the Matthew Shepard and James Byrd Jr. Hate Crimes Prevention Act, and it was signed into law that same year by President Barack Obama. The law requires the U.S. attorney general to provide assistance for the criminal investigation of felonies motivated by prejudice. This prejudice can be based on the perceived or actual race, color, religion, national origin, gender, sexual orientation, gender identity, or disability of the victim. The act also eliminates the prerequisite that the victim be engaging in a federally protected act such as voting or going to school; gives federal authorities power to investigate hate crimes that are not pursued by local authorities; provides $5 million annually for funding in the fiscal years from 2010 through 2012 to assist state and local agencies and tribal jurisdictions in paying for investigation and prosecution of hate crimes; and requires the FBI to track statistics on hate crimes against transgender people (statistics on other groups are already being tracked).

Hate Crime Laws in the European Union

The European Union has been in existence only since 1993. It does not yet have one overriding hate crime law for all its members, although negotiations have been ongoing for many years. Many of the member states, especially France, do have very strict hate crime laws of their own. However, the EU does have a "Framework Decision on Racism and Xenophobia," dated April 19, 2007, which states that certain acts should be punished by a maximum of one to three years of imprisonment, including:

- Publicly inciting to violence or hatred, against a group of persons or a member of such a group defined by reference to race, color, religion, descent, or national or ethnic origin
- Publicly condoning, denying, or grossly trivializing crimes of genocide, crimes against humanity, and war crimes
- Crimes directed against a group of persons or a member of such a group defined by reference to race, color, religion, descent, or national or ethnic origin

These rules set the minimum standard for EU states and do not rule out adding other protections, such as those for gay and lesbian citizens, to a country's laws.

In March 2009, the European Union Fundamental Rights Agency's report on "Homophobia and Discrimination on Grounds of Sexual Orientation and Gender Identity in the EU Member States" noted the significance of reporting activities: "Member States should consider developing simple and inclusive operational definitions of hate crime . . . In addition, effective tools should be developed to facilitate reporting, such as self-report forms and third party reporting facilities." In addition, the Ministerial Council of the Organization for Security and Cooperation in Europe adopted a "Decision on Combating Hate Crime" in December 2009, requesting participating member states to "collect, maintain and make public, reliable data and statistics in sufficient detail on hate crimes and violent manifestations of intolerance" and to "encourage victims to report hate crimes, recognizing that under-reporting of hate crimes prevents States from devising efficient policies."

Free Speech or Hate Crime?

One of the biggest conflicts in writing hate crime laws is in drawing the line between speech and action. For example, if someone sets up a giant swastika (a Nazi-era symbol of hatred toward Jews and other targeted minority groups) in his or her own yard, it is free speech. But it can also be seen as a way of intimidating Jews or other minorities who live in that neighborhood.

In some European countries, free speech is less of a protected right than in the United States, affecting how their hate crime laws are written. In the United States, the Constitution sets up strong protections for all speech, even objectionable and offensive speech. But if speech is used to harass, intimidate, or ruin a reputation with false accusations, then it can be restricted. Deciding when hate speech crosses the line into hate crime can be challenging for judges and lawmakers to determine.

Someone desecrated the Grand Synagogue in central Israel with a swastika. Countries around the world have been strengthening their legislation to prosecute hate crimes, especially laws that help protect religious rights.

Hate Crimes That Exploded into Genocide

When a country or a region dissolves into chaos or civil war, hate crime usually rises as well. Sometimes, it will mushroom into full-blown genocide, or the attempt to massacre an entire group of people. The slaughter of the Tutsi in Rwanda by the Hutu in 1994, the murder of Kosovar Albanians in the 1990s, and the ongoing attempt by the Sudanese government to wipe out the non-Arab peoples of Darfur in western Sudan are all attempts at ethnic-based genocide.

Of course, sometimes it is not chaos but calculation that makes a government choose genocide. The Holocaust of World War II was carried out by Nazi Germany through a highly organized government agenda. But although anti-Semitism had existed before the war broke out, the stress of war made it easier for the German government to justify imprisoning and murdering the Jewish population. Historically, crimes of hate also increase during times of stress, upheaval, and social change.

In July 2010, Canada's Ontario Provincial Police charged a Canadian extremist with promoting genocide. The extremist supposedly called for the "extermination" of Jews in Canada and other Western countries on various postings over the Internet. According to Ontario's *National Post*, the extremist was charged with "willfully promoting hatred and advocating or promoting genocide against an identifiable group." It is the first time such a case has been filed in Canada. The extremist fled the country and hid in Bangladesh after the police began investigating his use of the Internet to incite violence. The authorities believe he is still on the run.

two

HOW WERE HATE CRIMES BROUGHT TO THE PUBLIC EYE?

The horrific deaths of James Byrd Jr. in Jasper, Texas, in 1998 and Matthew Shepard in the same year put hate crimes in the spotlight. Whatever the debate over hate crime laws, no one could argue that the deaths of these two victims were motivated by anything but prejudice and fear. Byrd, an African American, was dragged to death down a 3-mile (4.8-kilometer) stretch of rural road by three white men, who chained Byrd by the ankles to the bumper of their pickup truck. He had accepted a ride from one of the men, whom he knew. Byrd's remains were found scattered along a winding path among pine trees. There was no motive for his murder other than the color of his skin. Matthew Shepard, a gay man, was killed by two men who pretended to be gay and offered him a ride in their car. They then beat him severely and tied him to a fence, leaving him to die. He didn't know his attackers.

These people are holding a candlelight vigil for Matthew Shepard, a gay student at the University of Wyoming who was savagely attacked and left to die tied to a fence.

The outrage following these two gruesome crimes and the publicity surrounding the trials made many more Americans aware that hate crimes were still a very real problem in the United States. The term "hate crimes" actually began being used in the 1980s when a wave of attacks against Jews and immigrants in Europe was launched by some neo-Nazi groups, who desecrated cemeteries, spray-painted homes with Nazi symbols and racist slurs, and published newsletters and books blaming immigrants such as Pakistanis for society's problems.

In 1925, hooded members of the Ku Klux Klan encircle a burning cross and U.S. flag during an initiation ceremony. After the enactment of the Civil Rights Act of 1964, law enforcement agencies vigorously prosecuted hate-based organizations.

The FBI Pursues the Ku Klux Klan

The FBI has been investigating what we now call "hate crimes" since the 1920s, when it opened its first case against the Ku Klux Klan (KKK), a secret society that advocates white supremacy. According to the FBI's Web site, by 1922, the KKK had grown so powerful that the governor of Louisiana begged the FBI to intervene. His message read: "Please help, the Ku Klux Klan has grown so powerful in my state that it effectively controls the northern half. It has already kidnapped, tortured, and killed two people who opposed it . . . and it has threatened many more." At this time, however, there were no hate crime or civil rights acts that could give the FBI jurisdiction to come in and prosecute the Klan.

What the FBI finally did was arrest one of the KKK's main organizers, Edward Young Clarke, for violating a minor transportation law, the Mann Act. From then on, the FBI regarded the Klan as dangerous domestic terrorists, which restricted the racist group's power. Still, it was many years before they could actually be prosecuted for hate crimes. Especially in the South, horrible crimes against African Americans, such as lynchings and cross burnings, were often ignored by local lawmakers. It wasn't until the civil rights movement of the 1950s and 1960s, and the passage of the Civil Rights Act of 1964 in particular, that racially motivated crimes moved to center stage and began to be seriously prosecuted. From then until the present day, membership in hate-based organizations such as the Klan has moved out of the mainstream and become largely unacceptable to most Americans.

A History of Hate Crimes in America

Discrimination in the United States didn't just happen to African Americans. The phrase "a Chinaman's chance"—meaning no chance whatsoever—was coined in the nineteenth century. It referred to the ways that Chinese immigrants were often falsely convicted of crimes before sham juries. Many immigrants, including the Irish, Italians, Jews, and others, were often killed in ethnic riots or falsely convicted of crimes, or suffered other injustices. Many were killed by assailants who were never prosecuted, much less convicted. Given that many minorities were not allowed to vote, hold office, or work in many professions, there were very few ways to change public attitudes regarding how they were treated.

However, hate groups like the Klan might have unintentionally set the United States on the path toward civil rights laws and hate crime laws. As they had in Louisiana, the Klan tried to seize power in other places in the United States, such as Texas and California. They used domestic terrorist tactics such as intimidating local officials, kidnapping, arson, and assault against certain whites whom they saw as enemies. It was in response to these actions as well as the KKK's racial violence that the U.S. government passed the Civil Rights Act of 1871, also known as the Ku Klux Klan Act of 1871. This act gave African Americans the right to sue in court for abuses committed against them by the Klan or other groups. At the time, it was seldom enforced, but it later became the basis for other civil rights laws, and it still remains in effect today.

Louisiana's Jena Six

In the high school of the small Louisiana town of Jena in September 2006, it was an unwritten rule that only white students could sit under a particular shade tree. That month, a black student asked permission from school administrators to sit under it as well. School officials told that student and other black students to sit wherever they wanted.

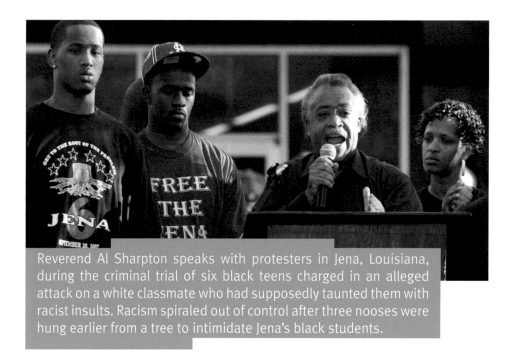

Reverend Al Sharpton speaks with protesters in Jena, Louisiana, during the criminal trial of six black teens charged in an alleged attack on a white classmate who had supposedly taunted them with racist insults. Racism spiraled out of control after three nooses were hung earlier from a tree to intimidate Jena's black students.

The next day, three nooses, in the school colors, were hanging from the same tree. It was a clear reference to the practice of lynching and an obvious reaction to the black students' actions. Jena's high school principal found that three white students were responsible and recommended expulsion. However, the white superintendent of schools decided to give the students a suspension only, saying that the nooses were "a youthful stunt."

In response, Jena's black students organized a sit-in under the tree. Tensions remained high. On Monday, December 4, 2006, a white student got into a fight with some black students after allegedly making racist taunts. The white student was taken to the hospital, treated, and released, and reportedly attended a social function later that evening.

As a result of this incident, six black Jena students were arrested and charged with attempted second-degree murder. All six were expelled from school. On the morning of the trial, the district attorney reduced the charges from attempted second-degree murder to second-degree aggravated battery and conspiracy. Aggravated battery in Louisiana law demands the attack be with a dangerous weapon. The prosecutor was allowed to argue to the jury that the tennis shoes worn by one of the students, Mychal Bell, could be considered a dangerous weapon.

Eventually, Bell pleaded guilty to second-degree battery and served eighteen months in jail. In June 2009, all five of the other students pleaded no contest to the charge of simple battery. The court found the students guilty as charged. They were fined, had to pay restitution to the white student's family, and sentenced to seven days of unsupervised probation.

What is remarkable about Jena is not the initial hate crime—the hanging of the nooses in order to intimidate Jena's black students. It is the aftermath that shows how hate crimes can flourish in an atmosphere of racism and unspoken discrimination. The fights between black and white students could not take place without the larger problem of racism in local law enforcement and even school administration. Hate crimes don't occur in a vacuum. As in Jena, they often happen because a group that is being discriminated against questions the way things are and, in questioning the status quo, comes to be seen as a threat.

Ten Great Questions to Ask Your Teacher

1 What are the most common types of hate crimes?

2 How often are hate crimes reported in our community?

3 While at school, who is the very first person I should report a hate crime to?

4 Who commits hate crimes?

5 How can I learn more about other cultures and religions?

6 Are there more hate crimes against religions today because of wars in the Middle East and Africa?

7 What is the first thing I should do if I am receiving threatening and hateful messages over the Internet?

8 What other reasons are there for hate crimes other than fear and ignorance?

9 What can I do to reduce bullying or hate crimes at my school?

10 What should I do if I witness a hate crime as a bystander?

Three

HOW DOES HATE CRIME HAPPEN?

What causes a human being to decide that another human being deserves to be treated with violence because, due to the person's skin color, religion, ethnicity, gender, or sexual orientation, he or she is perceived as different? There is no one simple answer, but there are many theories. Some of the more interesting theories are those described by journalist and author David Berreby in his book *Us and Them: Understanding Your Tribal Mind.*

According to Berreby, all social animals, including humans, know the difference between those who are their "kind," their kin, and those who aren't. The difference is that for animals, it is an instinct only—mother dogs guard their puppies, lions stay with their pride. But unlike animals, human beings can decide who belongs in their kinship group. They can switch religions, disown a blood relation, swap citizenship, move to a new country, or change their political party. Even if individuals share a race, they may not think of themselves as part of the same group. Many Americans are white, but they would not all consider themselves kin. They would be more likely to first call themselves Republicans, or Catholics, or members of the Smith family. Which of these kin groups is most important varies by person. Some people think religious affiliation is more important than skin color. Others think one's nationality or political views are more important to entry into a social or kin group.

When one group decides another group is "not our kind" according to Berreby, they often also decide that all the people of the outside group are alike and lump them together. "All Asians are good at math" and "white people can't dance" are common versions of this kind of thinking, which is called stereotyping.

"Not Our Kind"

To stereotype someone else, a person has to overlook both what makes that person unique and what makes that person no different from him- or herself. Because we all think of ourselves as "human," people who are "not our kind" can, in our own minds, seem less than completely human. This way of thinking is called "othering." You can see it at work in the propaganda used by the Nazis during World War II, which compared Jews to animals and monsters. During the eighteenth and nineteenth centuries in the United States, enslaved African Americans were widely

> When one group of people stereotypes another, they lump them together without any regard for individual differences. Stereotypes can affect important characteristics of a person's life, including educational expectations.

considered not quite human. They were classified as a type of animal and certainly were not considered as equals with white Americans. Native Americans were treated very similarly, as were various other ethnic groups

Throughout history, women, too, have often been considered less intelligent, talented, or rational than men. They were denied rights and privileges on the grounds that they were not capable of taking care of themselves or others.

People who have disabilities, also, have suffered terrible treatment historically. Often, the "able-bodied" around them believed they were demon-possessed, cursed, or sinful. They feared people with disabilities and often killed or tortured them, especially those with mental illnesses.

Seeing any group of people as less than human has one terrible result—it becomes much easier psychologically for other people to mistreat them. Such treatment has been repeated many times around the world and throughout history when one group has decided to make war on another, mistreats and exploits them, or oppresses them.

These demonstrators shout against same-sex marriages at an anti-gay rally in California. Some people, who are contributing to hate crimes, target gay people as the cause of certain social instability in the United States.

The legacy of this thinking lives on in all forms of hate crime. Nearly all those who commit these crimes will maintain that the ones they hurt are not like themselves and do not deserve protection or consideration. They will claim that they are dangerous monsters who must be stopped.

A Changing Society

Another force that contributes to hate crimes is social instability. This means a group of people may fear that their traditions or religious beliefs are dying out because of the way their society is changing. In response, the threatened group will often lash out at anyone whom they blame for causing that change. This kind of reaction is at work in many hate crimes committed against women and gays and lesbians, groups whose desire for equality has had a profound impact on U.S. society. Some men and women feel that the rise in the U.S. divorce rate and other social changes are bad for the United States and that feminism and gay and lesbian equality movements are to blame. They may target highly visible gay people or successful women with hate mail, the creation of derogatory Web sites, protests at their home or work, or stalking and violence.

A Changing Economy

Another kind of instability is economic. In the United States, this often results in violence or prejudice against immigrant groups, who are blamed for taking low-paying jobs and keeping all wages down. Although Mexican immigrants are the current targets of choice, in the past, Irish, Italians, eastern Europeans, and others have been blamed for similar reasons. As those groups became assimilated into American culture, new ethnic groups would come under fire for taking low-paying jobs from "real Americans" who were not willing to work for the low wages accepted by new immigrants.

Ironically, several studies show that the work of illegal immigrants has little effect on overall American wages, according to the *New York Times*. One study showed that:

> Across the entire labor force, the effect of illegal immigrants was zero, because the presence of uneducated immigrants actually increased the earnings of more educated workers, including high

school graduates. For instance, higher-skilled workers could hire foreigners at low wages to mow their lawns and care for their children, freeing time for these workers to earn more. And businesses that exist because of the availability of cheap labor might also need to employ managers.

All the same, new or illegal immigrants are highly visible because they often lack language skills and live in substandard housing, working low-wage service jobs that most Americans are not willing to take, such as janitors and cooks. Their high visibility and low status makes it easy for them to be "othered" and condemned as unintelligent, lazy, or even dangerous.

Activists rally against Arizona's immigration law that was enacted in 2010. The legislation allows law enforcement officials to stop and question suspected illegal immigrants.

People Who Commit Hate Crimes

According to the American Psychological Association (APA), most hate crimes are committed by:

> otherwise law-abiding young people who see little wrong with their actions . . . the main determinant appears to be personal prejudice . . . most likely rooted in an environment that disdains someone who is "different" or sees that difference as threatening. One expression of this prejudice is the perception that society sanctions attacks on certain groups . . . Extreme hate crimes tend to be committed by people with a history of antisocial behavior.

Hate crimes are the extreme end of prejudice. A great many people can and do hold prejudices against groups based on religion, race, gender, or other factors without ever acting violently on them. But the more accepted and normal discrimination against a group is, the more likely it is that some members of that group will be targeted.

The bad news is, as various groups fight to achieve equality in society, some of those who don't wish them to succeed will make attempts to strike out at them. The good news is that the outlook for many groups who are discriminated against has been getting better over the last several decades, as they have claimed their legal rights and fought to create new freedoms.

Myths and Facts

Most hate crimes involve sexual orientation bias.

Fact: ➡ According to the FBI's hate crime statistics for 2009, the majority of hate crimes were prompted by racial bias (48.5 percent), followed by religious bias (19.7 percent), and then sexual orientation bias (18.5 percent).

Hatred of others who are different is normal and instinctive.

Fact: ➡ Hatred of other groups is a taught, conscious behavior, rooted in fear and ignorance, and sometimes inflamed by people who want to use fear of "outsiders" to gain more power.

Race is a genetic difference.

Fact: ➡ Race is not a true distinguishing difference as species is—it is a genetic variation. There is no such thing as a pure race, just people who have more or less of certain genetic traits, all of which are outward and physical. Brain development and intelligence are no different among races, although they may be affected by lack of access to nutrition and education.

four

WHO HAVE BEEN VICTIMS OF HATE CRIMES IN AMERICA?

Hate crimes in the United States are influenced by fear and hatred of othered groups, social instability, and economic instability. The following are some of the more noteworthy outbreaks of hate crime against various groups of people living in the United States.

American Indians

Historically speaking, Native American groups have not suffered hate crimes so much as a near-genocide of their people coinciding with the arrival of European settlers. Not all of the deaths were intentional, as the germs that Europeans brought to the New World may have killed more Native Americans than any warfare that took place

President Barack Obama speaks before signing the Tribal Law and Order Act of 2010, which strengthens tribal law enforcement and helps victims of sexual assaults. One in three Native American women will be raped in their lifetime, according to the Justice Department, and non–Native American men commit most of the cases.

Those old wounds, however, remain raw in the United States, and periodically violence will break out against the remaining members of Native American tribes. According to the FBI's hate crime statistics for 2009, there were 3,816 single-bias hate crimes that were racially motivated, and of these offenses, 2.2 percent were motivated by anti-American Indian and Alaskan Native biases.

In 2010, Attorney General Eric Holder announced that the U.S. Department of Justice would be instituting broad reforms to improve public safety in tribal communities. According to government statistics, one in three Native American women will suffer a sexual assault in her lifetime. A confusion of laws that govern reservation lands and state police jurisdiction has left loopholes that make it very difficult to convict anyone who commits violent crimes on a reservation. Although some assaults are committed by Native American men, 86 percent of the assaults on Native American women on reservations are committed by non–Native American men, most of them white. Almost none of the assailants have ever been caught or convicted. Attorney General Holder acknowledged that fixing these problems will be challenging, but he said he is committed to working toward solving them.

African Americans

Like Native Americans, African Americans have suffered through a long and tragic history stemming from the slave trade that brought their ancestors to America in the eighteenth century. The brutality and injustice that many generations of slaves endured improved only slightly when President Abraham Lincoln signed the Emancipation Proclamation. It was not until the civil rights movement of the 1960s that true equality began to be possible for many African Americans.

On Sunday, June 7, 1998, churchgoers in the small town of Jasper, Texas, were horrified to find the dismembered body of James Byrd Jr., which had been dumped on a little-used road. He had been dragged to death. Evidence at the scene pointed to Lawrence Brewer, a local white man. Because Brewer was known to be interested in white supremacist movements, the FBI decided to investigate the case as a civil rights crime. Eventually Brewer, John King, and Shawn Berry were convicted of the murder, and Brewer and King were sentenced to death. Although then-governor George W. Bush had resisted signing hate crime legislation, the next governor of Texas, Rick Perry, signed the James Byrd Jr. Hate Crimes Act into law in May 2001. In 2009, the Matthew Shepard and James Byrd Jr. Hate Crimes Prevention Act became a federal law when it was passed by the U.S. Congress and signed by President Barack Obama. The FBI reported in 2009 that 71.4 percent of the 3,816 single-bias racially motivated hate crimes committed that year were by people who had an anti-black bias.

The red circles on this road indicate where parts of James Byrd Jr.'s body were found in Jasper, Texas. The Texas governor signed the James Byrd Jr. Hate Crimes Act into state law in 2001. Eight years later, the federal government expanded it, and today it is a federal crime to assault people because of prejudice.

European Immigrants

All Americans except Native Americans came to the United States as immigrants. But historically, different immigrant groups have been blamed for crime, disease, and additional problems by other, longer-established groups who considered themselves "real" Americans. In the nineteenth and early twentieth centuries, signs such as "No Irish" could be found in numerous places of business, and strict laws governed how many members of every immigrant group could enter the United States. Preference was usually given to white northern Europeans, with groups such as Italians and eastern Europeans considered less desirable and more prone to "criminal" behavior.

In fact, in 1891, eleven Italians were lynched in New Orleans, Louisiana, provoking an outcry from the Italian government. Following the murder of the city's police commissioner, suspicion had fallen upon eleven Sicilian immigrants, who were put on trial but were declared not guilty. A mob then stormed the jail, dragged the immigrants out, and murdered them.

Latinos

In the spring of 2011, the Southern Poverty Law Center (SPLC) released an intelligence report titled "The Year in Hate & Extremism, 2010," warning of an upswing in organized groups committing hate crimes. In 2010, the SPLC said it counted 1,002 active hate groups in its latest tally, up from 932 in 2009.

Students at Rutgers University write words of sympathy at a memorial for fellow student Tyler Clementi. Clementi committed suicide after he was allegedly harassed by his roommate and a friend for being gay.

Among its findings was a link between anti-immigrant activism and a rise in hate crimes against Latinos. It cited FBI statistics that show that 692 people were victimized by anti-Latino hate crimes in 2009. "The immigration debate has turned ugly, and the result has been a growth in white supremacist hate groups and anti-Latino hate crime," said Mark Potok, director of the law center's Intelligence Project. "The majority of anti-Latino hate crimes are carried out by people who think they're attacking immigrants, and very likely undocumented immigrants."

Potok said that many new anti-immigration groups have appeared in the border states of California, Texas, and Arizona, where illegal immigration has been a difficult issue. One shocking example includes a case in Maricopa County, Arizona, where Juan Varela, a Mexican American, was killed and his brother was shot in the neck by Gary Thomas Kelley, a neighbor. According to the U.S. attorney's office, Kelley, who was allegedly drunk at the time, pointed a gun at Varela and said, "Hurry up and go back to Mexico or you're gonna die." Varela's family had lived in Arizona for several generations. Kelley claimed that he was defending himself after Varela supposedly kicked him. In February 2011, a judge ruled the murder trial of Kelley a mistrial, after the jury was unable to reach a verdict.

Immigration fears, according to the SPLC, seem to be driven by a slow economy and by panic over the projection that by 2050, whites will no longer be the majority in the United States because of immigration.

Lesbians and Gays

On May 13, 1988, Rebecca Wight and her partner, Claudia Brenner, were shot by Stephen Roy Carr while hiking and camping along the Appalachian Trail. Wight was killed, but Brenner survived. Carr claimed that he became enraged by the fact that the two were lesbians. He did not know the victims and decided to attack them only after he realized they were lesbians. Brenner, who went on to become an anti-gay-violence speaker, said later, "I never thought that you could be killed for being gay. I knew about taunts and harassment, and that's what I thought of when someone said anti-gay. I never thought it happened to women. I never thought it was a matter of life and death." According to the FBI's Hate Crime Statistics for 2009, there were 1,436 hate crime offenses based on sexual orientation, 15 percent of which were classified as anti-female homosexual bias. Almost 56 percent of the 1,436 hate crimes were the result of anti-male homosexual bias.

In September 2010, Tyler Clementi, an eighteen-year-old freshman at Rutgers University in New Jersey killed himself after, authorities said, his college roommate and another student used a Webcam to spy on and stream video of Clementi's sexual encounter with another man. The two Rutgers students, who have since left Rutgers, have been charged with two counts of invasion of privacy. A New Jersey grand jury indicted the roommate, Dharun Ravi, on hate-crime charges, which could lead to a sentence of at least five to ten years in prison, if he is convicted. In all, Ravi faces fifteen charges, including three counts of tampering with physical evidence (he deleted a Twitter post that alerted others to watch a second video of Clementi, replacing it with a post that was intended to mislead investigators in the case). Legal scholars are watching the case closely because it will send a message to other prosecutors who are handling similar cases in other states about the dangerous consequences of this kind of bias crime. In March 2011, U.S. senator Frank Lautenberg and U.S. representative Rush Holt reintroduced legislation in both houses of Congress that would require colleges and universities that receive federal money to adopt policies that prohibit harassment based on a student's sexual orientation, race, gender, and other factors. Called the Tyler Clementi Higher Education Anti-Harassment Act, the law, if it is enacted, would also provide funding for colleges to establish or expand programs to prevent harassment.

Women

In March 2007, Kathy Sierra, a popular Web developer, author, and blogger, canceled an appearance at an important technical conference. On her blog, she wrote:

> As I type this, I am supposed to be in San Diego, delivering a workshop at the ETech conference. But I'm not. I'm at home, with the doors locked, terrified. For the last four weeks, I've been getting death threat comments on this blog. But that's not what pushed me over the edge. What finally did was some disturbing threats of violence . . . posted on two other blogs . . . blogs authored and/or owned by a group that includes prominent bloggers.

Actress Salma Hayek (*center*) marches with other women to the U.S. Capitol to champion the increase in funding of the Violence Against Women Act. Supporters of the act dressed as brides in honor of Gladys Ricart, who was killed by a former boyfriend on the day of her wedding to another man.

Misogyny, or hatred of women, is one of the most common forms of hatred, making violence against women distressingly common around the world. In the United States, the Violence Against Women Act (VAWA) of 1994 has provided more than $4 billion to combating domestic violence and sexual assault. As a group, women remain the primary victims of relationship violence and partner violence, including stalking, death threats, and murder. The VAWA was reauthorized by Congress in 2000 and 2005, and its current authorization expires in 2011.

Until the Matthew Shepard and James Byrd Jr. Hate Crimes Prevention Act was enacted in late 2009, bias attack statistics against women were not being kept by the federal government and many state governments because they excluded women as a class in their hate crime laws and statutes, according to the Leadership Conference on Civil and Human Rights.

Religious Bias

At various times in U.S. history, some religious groups have been persecuted or considered less desirable or tolerable than others. The constitutional protections against religious discrimination have not kept some people from using religion as an excuse to commit hate crimes. Ironically, many who fled to the American colonies to escape religious persecution, such as the Puritans, would then try to persecute others who did not follow their ways once they arrived. It was up to reformers like Roger Williams, who founded the colony of Rhode Island, to attempt to practice true religious tolerance at the social and governmental levels.

Vandals defaced a mosque with anti-Muslim graffiti in Detroit, Michigan. After the 9/11 terrorist attacks in the United States, many American Muslims feared there would be an increase in bias attacks against them.

After the September 11, 2001, terrorist attacks on the United States, people around the world—including many in countries like Iran and Saudi Arabia—mourned the senseless destruction and loss of life caused by the radical Islamic hijackers. Many in the United States worried that some Americans would try to retaliate against anyone they associated with the 9/11 attackers—anyone who "looked Muslim," or Arabic or Middle Eastern. And indeed, in the months after the attack, several Sikh men, who wear a distinctive headdress, were harassed and assaulted, despite the fact that Sikhs are not Muslim and were not involved in the 9/11 attacks. According to the FBI's hate crime statistics in 2009, there were 1,376 hate crimes motivated by religious bias—9.3 percent were anti-Islamic and 70.1

percent were anti-Jewish. As reported in the *San Francisco Sentinel*, the Center for Security Policy released a revision of their study, "Religious Bias Crimes 2000–2009: Muslim, Jewish and Christian Victims," in April 2011, saying that hate crimes against Muslim Americans, "measured by the categories of incidents, offenses or victims, have remained relatively low with a downward trend since 2001, and are significantly less than the numbers of bias crimes against Jewish victims." According to the center's review, Jewish victims of bias crimes outnumbered Muslim victims by more than eight to one.

People Who Have Disabilities

Since it was passed in 1990, the Hate Crime Statistics Act requires the U.S. attorney general to collect data on crimes committed because of a victim's race, religion, disability, sexual orientation, or ethnicity. According to the statistics collected since then, hate crimes against the disabled have been low; only around 1.5 percent as of 2009, for example. However, some advocates for people with disabilities say these statistics are inaccurate.

University of California-Berkeley researcher Mark Sherry, author of the 2003 report "Don't Ask, Tell, or Respond: Silent Acceptance of Disability Hate Crimes," maintains that most hate crimes against the disabled either go unreported or are not prosecuted as hate crimes. He believes many crimes are never reported because the victim has no way of contacting the police without help or because the victim is being abused by the person caring for him or her.

According to Jack Levin, a professor of sociology and criminology at Northeastern University in Boston, Massachusetts, in his article "The Invisible Hate Crime," on Miller-McCune.com in March 2011, "Attacks on people with disabilities are often overlooked because many people are not aware of the extreme vulnerability to maltreatment that accompanies such disorders as cerebral palsy, autism, multiple sclerosis, learning disabilities and mental illness—even though according to anonymous victim accounts from the Bureau of Justice Statistics, the 54 million Americans with disabilities experience serious violence at a rate nearly twice that of the general population."

five

ARE HATE CRIMES A PROBLEM GLOBALLY?

As in the United States, hate crimes around the world tend to be fueled by fear of outsiders, social instability, and economic instability. Unlike the United States, many countries have not considered themselves friendly to immigrants or as a "melting pot" of many nationalities. Nations much older than the United States may have histories of racial, national, or religious conflicts that stretch back for centuries, making the rooting out of old prejudices and hostilities a harder task. Some grudges and prejudices may go as far back as conflicts fought in the Middle Ages or even earlier. Others are more recent, a result of fights over resources or over social change.

Russia and Hate Crimes

Since the fall of the Soviet Union in 1991, its former states, including Russia, have suffered through a severe

Ultranationalists march in Moscow, Russia, during a May Day rally. Battles against racism and xenophobia continue to be fought in Russia today.

set of economic and social upheavals. Russia, in particular, has had to deal with the rise of organized crime and the challenge of corrupt officials from the old regime still seeking to cling to power. Unemployment and poverty have been widespread. Unsurprisingly, one of the results of this chaos is a surge in hate crime. In 2009, 71 people were killed and more than 333 others injured in racially motivated hate crime attacks, according to the Russian human rights group Sova. These numbers are down from the previous year, partly because of amended legislation, lengthy criminal trials, and improved police techniques. In spite of the decrease in hate crimes, Sova noted that there was an increasing volume of xenophobic propaganda, especially among right-wing political youth groups. In 2010, as reported by Sova, there were more than 400 people who became victims of racists and xenophobes, 37 of whom were killed.

Europe and Hate Crimes

In many European countries, a large influx of immigrants from Asian and African countries has had a profound social impact. Language, cuisine, music, religion, and culture have all been affected in the traditionally white, Christian countries of western Europe. For the most part, these nations have adjusted to and even welcomed these immigrants as new citizens, although racist attitudes persist. Muslims, especially, have faced additional pressures after the September 11, 2001, terrorist attacks in the United States and other attacks in Spain and Britain.

In November 2010, the Democracy and Human Rights branch of the Organization for Security in Cooperation in Europe released its yearly hate crime report, reviewing events and offenses that took place in 2009. Among the member states issuing statistics were the following: the United Kingdom reported 52,102 hate crimes; Spain said there had been a large decrease in that country, from 224 in 2007 to 23 in 2009; Germany recorded 4,583; Italy had 142 incidents; Poland reported 209 offenses; and Greece reported only 2 hate crime offenses.

According to Jack Levin, who has written extensively on hate crime in Europe and America, one remaining problem is that "the police in Europe haven't been trained to recognize hate crime." Although incidents like these remain far too common, vocal and active immigrant and ethnic-rights groups in Europe have made many gains in protecting groups from hate crime.

The Caste Conflict in India

One of the oldest features of Indian culture is its caste system. Many sociologists believe the caste system in India originated as a way of dividing labor, keeping social control, and maintaining order. Within it, the people of India are divided into five main castes. The first four are the Brahmins, the Kshatriyas, the Vaishyas, and the Sudras, who are required to serve the other three. Within these four, there are more than three thousand subcastes, or *jatis*. The fifth and lowest caste is the "Untouchables," who have historically been forced to live in their own enclaves, not allowed to touch or talk to members of higher castes or even walk on the same path as them. Today, in India, the Untouchables call themselves Dalits, which means "Broken People." There are almost 200 million Dalits in India alone and at least another 60 million around the world.

According to the Web site DalitFoundation.org, "untouchability" was formally outlawed by the constitution of India in 1950. However the Dalits are still often denied access to community property such as water sources and public land, as well as equal opportunities in education and employment. The Dalits have made many gains and elected a Dalit, K. R. Narayanan, as India's tenth president in 1997. But not all Dalits have benefited, and they are often still the targets of hate crime. The National Campaign on Dalit Human Rights reported that in September 2007, ten Dalits were murdered by lynching in the village of Dhelpurwa, allegedly for being "thieves." A single survivor had serious injuries. In 2009, the National Crime Records Bureau in India reported that according to government statistics, there were 33,594 crimes committed against Dalits.

During a demonstration in New Delhi, India, activists protest an attack against Dalits in which more than fifty Dalit homes were burned.

Darfur's Victims

Three small states on the western edge of Sudan, in Africa, make up the region of Darfur. Since 2003, there has been intense fighting in this region between the government of Sudan, with some Arabic tribal allies, and rebels based in the Darfur region. As many as 300,000 people have died from the effects of war, starvation, and disease since the conflict began. The conflict may have started because of the spreading of the desert, which forced nomadic groups into the Darfur farmlands looking for water for their animals. A famine in the 1980s killed thousands of people, and its aftereffects are still being felt.

Sudan's government has been brutal in its crackdown on the Darfur people, killing witnesses and protesters and threatening to treat UN peacekeeping forces as invaders. In 2010, the UN reported that there were at least 2.7 million people who had fled from their homes because of the violence. Worse, the Sudanese government had committed crimes against humanity, including murder, torture, mass rape, summary executions, and arbitrary detention of many civilians and anyone they perceived as aiding the rebels. While the UN hasn't yet called what's happening a genocide, it is clear that what is happening are hate crimes on a massive scale.

The stories of Darfur's victims are heartbreaking. A brave survivor of rape and assault, Awatif Ahmed Salih, spoke in 2007 to the *Times*, an English newspaper. At the age of sixteen, she was kidnapped and assaulted over a three-day span before being rescued. Like her, thousands of women have been raped during the conflict as a way of breaking the spirit of the Darfur people. The violence is designed to drive them away from their homes.

Refugees from Darfur await tents for shelter in a camp in Chad in 2004. The United Nations reported in 2010 that there were close to three million people who had fled violence in the Darfur region of Sudan.

Habiba Mohamed Elhag, the women's officer of Awatif's town, said of those who assaulted Darfur's women, "They did it because they want to destroy the kindness and the hearts of the women." Because there is a stigma to rape in her society, Awatif was told not to have her picture taken or to give her name to any reporters. She insisted, however, that her name and photograph be used. "I want you to use my true name because I have told you the truth of what happened. This will be a message to other women over the world to support the women here."

It is not clear what will become of the people of Darfur. Fights over scarce resources such as water and farmland are the hardest to resolve and the most likely to escalate into violence. Desperation over food, shelter, or other necessities feeds into the mind-set that makes it easy to commit hate crimes. This, in turn, can lead to all-out warfare and genocide. And if tension already exists between groups because of their ethnic background (as in Darfur), then it becomes very difficult, though not impossible, to seek out peaceful resolutions.

six

WHAT ABOUT FUTURE HATE CRIME LAWS?

In the United States and around the world, the focus of hate crime laws is likely to continue evolving. More accurate reporting and statistics, education of all citizens and law enforcement, and new rulings in the judicial system will all affect the ways in which hate crime laws are created and enforced.

It's possible that new groups will need to seek protection. There is some evidence that the elderly and those with medical conditions such as HIV can be targeted for abuse or violence. On the other hand, as groups that were once targets become assimilated into the mainstream, crimes against them may drop off. While it can be very daunting to look at all the ways human beings have "othered" certain groups or targeted them for violence, it is also important to note how such a process can fade away.

Michael Magidson was found guilty of second-degree murder in a California courtroom for the death of Gwen Araujo, a transgender teen. He and another man were cleared of hate crime charges in the murder. The federal government has the authority to prosecute violent hate crimes, including those committed against transgender victims.

In *Us and Them*, David Berreby recounts the history of the Cagots, a class of people in French society who were considered much like Dalits in India—untouchable. They were allowed to work only in a few occupations, lived on the edges of towns and villages, had to wear special identifying marks on their clothes, married only among themselves, and even had separate entrances into churches. Like the Dalits, they were not genetically distinct in any way from their countrypeople, but they were restricted to a lower level of society. But after the French Revolution, the laws against them were abolished, and the customs of separation simply faded out.

This history shows us that the challenge of fighting the attitudes that lead to hate crimes, genocide, and discrimination lies in changing perceptions. And preferably, to do all of that without having to experience war and upheaval. Instead, tools like education, social stability, and a commitment to taking hate crime seriously create a more positive path to reaching this goal.

Hate crimes are some of the oldest types of crime and the hardest to fight. However, people of differing colors, sexual orientations, political beliefs, and religions can live together peacefully, if they feel invested in their society and not discriminated against. Fighting hate crime in the United States and abroad requires understanding its roots in the ways of thinking and in various cultures. It requires education that breaks down old ideas of racial and cultural animosity. Finally, it requires legislation and enforcement to take such crimes seriously, to offer sanctuary to those who are threatened, and to prosecute the offenders.

advocate To publicly recommend or support something.

anti-Semitism Hostility toward or prejudice against Jews or Judaism; discrimination against Jews.

assimilation The process by which a minority group adopts the customs and attitudes of the majority culture.

bias Prejudice in favor of or against one thing, person, or group compared with another, usually in a way considered to be unfair.

bigotry Having strong opinions, especially on politics, religion, or ethnicity, and refusing to accept different views.

civil rights In the United States, privileges and rights guaranteed by the United States Constitution and its amendments, as well as laws that guarantee fundamental freedoms to all individuals.

derogatory Something that is belittling, uncomplimentary, or scathing; something showing a critical or disrespectful attitude.

desecrate To treat something, such as a sacred place or thing, with violent discrespect; to violate.

discrimination The unfair treatment of one person or group, usually because of prejudice about race, ethnicity, age, religion, or gender.

Emancipation Proclamation The proclamation signed by President Abraham Lincoln on January 1, 1863, freeing the slaves in those Confederate territories still in rebellion against the Union.

ethnicity The fact or state of belonging to a social group that has a common national or cultural tradition.

felony A serious crime (such as murder or arson), punishable by prison terms of more than one year or by death.

feminism Belief in the social, political, and economic equality of the sexes.

genocide The systematic killing of all the people from a national, ethnic, or religious group, or an attempt to do this.

incite To stir up feelings in or provoke action by somebody.

intolerance An unwillingness or refusal to accept people who are different from you, or views, beliefs, or lifestyles that differ from your own.

lynching Putting a person to death, as by hanging, by mob action without legal sanction.

neo-Nazi A person who belongs to an organization whose beliefs are similar to the German Nazi Party; a person who has extreme racist or nationalist views.

prejudice A preformed opinion, usually an unfavorable one, based on insufficient knowledge, irrational feelings, or inaccurate stereotypes.

prerequisite An object, quality, or condition that is required as a prior condition for something else to happen.

prosecution The trial of someone in a court of law for a criminal offense.

Puritans Members of a group of English Protestants who in the sixteenth and seventeenth centuries advocated strict religious discipline and the simplification of the ceremonies and creeds of the Church of England.

restitution The return of something to its rightful owner; compensation for a loss, damage, or injury.

sham Something that is presented as being genuine but is not.

stalking Following or harassing another person in a way that would cause the person to fear injury or death, especially if violent threats are involved.

stereotype An oversimplified standardized image of a person or group.

transgender Identified with a gender other than the biological one a person is born with.

xenophobic Describing an intense or irrational dislike or fear of people from other countries.

American Civil Liberties Union (ACLU)

125 Broad Street, Eighteenth Floor

New York, NY 10004

(212) 549-2500

Web site: http://www.aclu.org

The ACLU works to extend rights to segments of the
U.S. population that have traditionally been denied
their rights, including Native Americans and other
people of color; lesbians, gay men, bisexuals, and
transgender people; women; mental-health patients;
prisoners; people with disabilities; and people living
in poverty.

Canadian Human Rights Commission

344 Slater Street, Eighth Floor

Ottawa, ON K1A 1E1

Canada

(888) 214-1090

Web site: http://www.chrc-ccdp.ca

This independent commission administers the Canadian
Human Rights Act and ensures compliance with the
Employment Equity Act, both of which guarantee the
principles of equal opportunity and nondiscrimination
throughout the federal jurisdiction of Canada.

Canadian Race Relations Foundation (Fondation canadienne
des relations raciales)
4576 Yonge Street, Suite 701
Toronto, ON M2N 6N4
Canada
(888) 240-4936
Web site: http://www.crr.ca
The Canadian Race Relations Foundation works to fight
    against racism in Canada.

Human Rights First
333 Seventh Avenue, Thirteenth Floor
New York, NY 10001-5108
(212) 845 5200
Web site: http://www.humanrightsfirst.org
Human Rights First is based in New York City and
    Washington, D.C., and works to build respect for human
    rights and the rule of law to help guarantee the dignity to
    which every person is entitled and to stop intolerance,
    tyranny, and violence.

LAMDA GLBT Community Services
216 South Ochoa Street
El Paso, TX 79901
For Hate-crime assistance: (206) 350-HATE (4283)
Web site: http://www.lambda.org
This group's mission is to work for full civil rights and self-
    respect for gay, lesbian, bisexual, and transgendered

people through education, youth advocacy, and anti-violence programs. There is also a Youth OUTreach organization link available on the Web site for youth issues guidance.

Leadership Conference on Civil Rights Education Fund (LCCREF)
1629 K Street NW, Tenth Floor
Washington, DC 20006
(202) 466-3434
Web site: http://www.civilrights.org/about/lccref
Founded in 1969 as the education and research arm of the civil rights coalition, the Leadership Conference on Civil Rights Education Fund (LCCREF) uses its research and education campaigns to promote an understanding of the need for national policies that support civil rights and social and economic justice.

Southern Poverty Law Center
400 Washington Avenue
Montgomery, AL 36104
(334) 956-8200
Web site: http://www.splcenter.org
The Southern Poverty Law Center is internationally known for its tolerance education programs, its legal victories against white supremacists, its tracking of hate groups, and winning justice for exploited workers, abused prison inmates, disabled children, and other victims of discrimination.

The Tolerance Foundation
180 René-Lévesque Boulevard East, Suite 420
Montreal, QC, H2X 1N6
Canada
(514) 842-4848
Web site: http://www.fondationtolerance.com
The Tolerance Foundation's mission is to prevent, inform, and
    raise awareness about the dangers inherent in intolerance,
    prejudice, exclusion, racism, and discrimination in all its forms.

Web Sites

Due to the changing nature of Internet links, Rosen Publishing
has developed an online list of Web sites related to the subject
of this book. This site is updated regularly. Please use this link
to access this list:

http://www.rosenlinks.com/faq/hate

Bartoletti, Susan Campbell. *They Called Themselves the K.K.K.: The Birth of an American Terrorist Group.* New York, NY: Houghton Mifflin, 2010.

Bordeau, Jamie. *Xenophobia: The Violence of Fear and Hate* (In the News). New York, NY: Rosen Publishing, 2009.

Bruce, Judith. *Hate Crimes* (Issues on Trial). Farmington Hills, MI: Greenhaven Press, 2009.

Bussey, Jennifer. *Hate Crimes* (History of Issues). Farmington Hills, MI: Greenhaven Press, 2007.

Coleman, Wim, and Pat Perrin. *Racism on Trial: From the Medgar Evers Murder Case to Ghosts of Mississippi* (Famous Court Cases That Became Movies). Berkeley Heights, NJ: Enslow Publishers, 2009.

Connors, Paul. *Hate Crimes* (Current Controversies). Farmington Hills, MI: Greenhaven Press, 2006.

Ehrenberg, Pamela. *Tillman County Fire.* Grand Rapids, MI: Eerdmans Books for Young Readers, 2009.

Gold, Susan Dudley. *Americans with Disabilities Act* (Landmark Legislation). Marshall Cavendish, 2010.

Hudson, David L., Jr. *Hate Crimes* (Point/Counterpoint). 2nd ed. New York, NY: Facts On File, Inc., 2009.

Merino, Noel. *Gender* (Issues on Trial). Farmington Hills, MI: Greenhaven Press, 2010.

Palmer, Bill. *Homophobia: From Social Stigma to Hate Crimes* (The Gallup's Guide to Modern Gay, Lesbian, and Transgender Lifestyle). Broomall, PA: Mason Crest Publishers, 2010.

Stewart, Mark. *The Indian Removal Act: Forced Relocation* (Snapshots in History). Minneapolis, MN: Compass Point Books, 2007.

Streissguth, Tom. *Hate Crimes* (Library in a Book). Rev. ed. New York, NY: Facts On File, Inc., 2009.

Uschan, Michael V. *Hate Crimes* (Hot Topics). Farmington Hills, MI: Lucent Books, 2007.

Volponi, Paul. *Response*. New York, NY: Viking Juvenile, 2009.

Willis, Laurie. *Hate Crimes* (Social Issues Firsthand). Farmington Hills, MI: Greenhaven Press, 2007.

Winters, Robert. *What Is a Hate Crime?* (At Issue). Farmington Hills, MI: Gale Cengage Learning, 2007.

About the Authors

Barbara Dunkell is a writer who resides in Yorktown Heights, New York.

Janell Broyles, a communications and publications professional, has written several books for young adults. She lives near Dallas, Texas.

Photo Credits

Cover Image Source/Getty Images; p. 5 Henrik Sorensen/Stone/ Getty Images; p. 8 Saul Loeb/AFP/Getty Images; p. 11 David Silverman/Getty Images; p. 14 Steve Liss/Time & Life Pictures/Getty Images; p. 15 Jack Benton/Archive Photos/Getty Images; pp. 18, 43 AFP/Getty Images; p. 23 Jetta Productions/Lifesize/Thinkstock; p. 24 David McNew/Getty Images; p. 26 Justin Sullivan/Getty Images; p. 30 Mandel Ngan/AFP/Getty Images; p. 32 Buck Kelly/Getty Images; p. 34 Emmanuel Dunand/AFP/Getty Images; p. 37 Tom Williams/CQ-Roll Call Group/Getty Images; p. 39 Bill Pugliano/ Getty Images; p. 46 Raveendran/AFP/Getty Images; p. 48 Scott Nelson/Getty Images; p. 51 © AP Images.

Photo Researcher: Karen Huang